Parrot's Sticker Book

Silver Dolphin
San Diego, California

Silver Dolphin

Silver Dolphin Books
An imprint of the Advantage Publishers Group
5880 Oberlin Drive, San Diego, CA 92121–4794
www.silverdolphinbooks.com

Illstration copyright © 2003 by Derek Matthews
Text and design copyright © 2003 by The Templar Company plc,
Pippbrook Mill, London Road, Dorking, Surrey, RH4 IJE, UK

ISBN 1–57145–945–6

Designed by Janie Louise Hunt and Caroline Reeves
Written by Beth Harwood and Dug Steer

1 2 3 4 5 07 06 05 04 03

Printed in Italy

About this book

It's time for some Snappy sticker fun! On the following pages, you can take a trip through the jolly jungle, dive beneath the ocean, or enjoy a day on the farm!

At the back of this book you will find over 200 colorful stickers! Use them to fill in the spaces in five fun, read—aloud, rhyming stories, or to complete the sticker activities that will also help you to learn to count and to recognize colors. You can even get creative and use your stickers to create some pictures of your own!

Meet Parrot and his friends

Join Parrot on a trip through the jolly jungle, take a dive in the deep blue sea with Dolphin, fly high with Toucan and his flock of feathered friends, spend a day on Snappy Farm with Pig, then look closely for Beetle and his bug friends!

Parrot and his friends are here to help you to count and to recognize colors!

Don't forget, you can have lots of fun with your stickers as you go through the book!

The Jolly Jungle

"Who is the king of the jungle?"

The colorful  said.

"The might know and tell us so!"

But he just shook his head.

The 🐒 had never seen him,

Nor had the 🐍 in the tree.

Find the stickers for the story.

6

But then we went to ask ,

Who pointed to where he might be.

On the way we saw a ,

And a  who hopped on the floor,

Until at last we met a big

Who said, "I'm the king!" with a roar.

Parrot's Pair

Two's company!
Can you find a friend
for each of these animals?

Now count
the animals.

1 2 3 4 5

Home Time!

The animal babies have been playing all day. Now they are tired and heading for home. Use your stickers to put each baby next to the right parent.

Which animals have one baby?
Which animals have two babies?

6   7   8   9   10

Jungle Colors

red

Parrot is **red**. He has been looking for other **red** things in the jungle. Fill this page with stickers to show all the **red** things you can find.

red berries

red lizard

red bird

red beetles

red flowers

Find the stickers to match the colors.

yellow
flowers

Snake is **yellow**.
She has been looking for other
yellow things in the jungle. Fill
this page with stickers to show
all the **yellow** things you
can find.

yellow
butterfly

yellow
bananas

yellow birds

yellow frog

Join Parrot for
some jungle fun!
Use your stickers to
create a lively jungle scene.

Diving with Dolphin

Little , won't you come

and dive down deep with me?

I want to see  swim

with  in the sea.

We'll have a game of hide-and-seek

with  below.

Find the stickers for the story.

We'll soon find of every sort

and see where go.

Perhaps we'll find a reef

where loves to roam.

And then we'll smile and say good-bye,

and turn to swim for home.

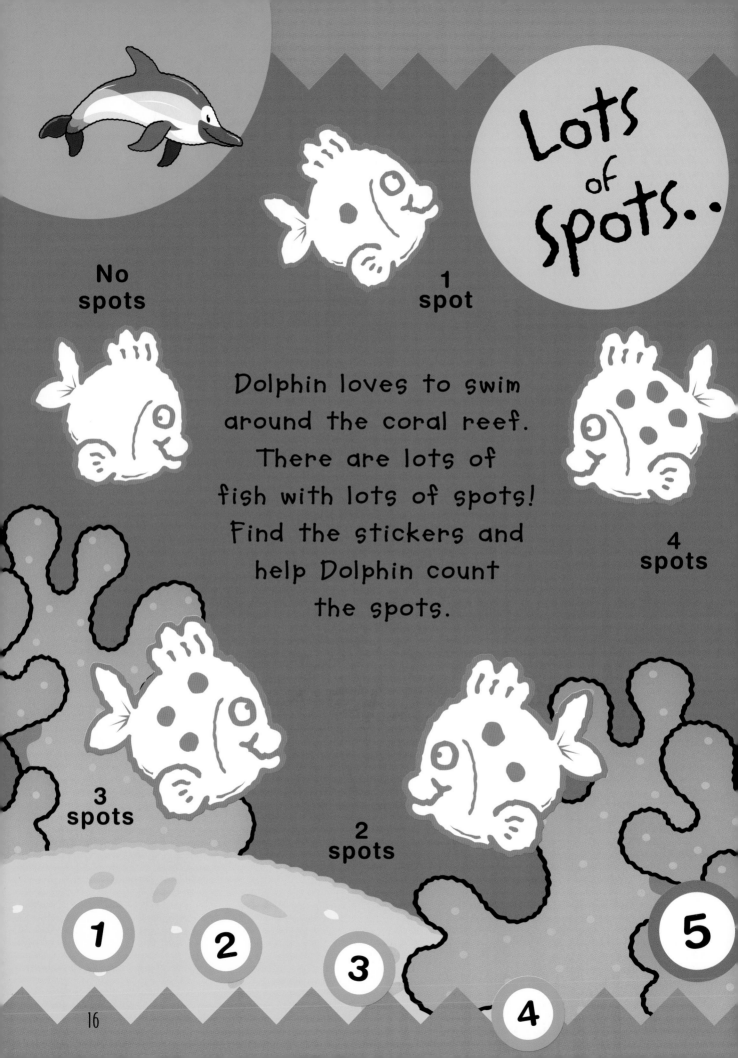

Lots of spots..

No spots

1 spot

Dolphin loves to swim around the coral reef. There are lots of fish with lots of spots! Find the stickers and help Dolphin count the spots.

4 spots

3 spots

2 spots

1 2 3 4 5

..and Lots of Yachts!

Add the stickers
and count all
the different
boats.

6   7   8   9   10

Dolphin Colors

green

Dolphin's favorite
colors are **blue** and **green**.
But he likes **red** and **yellow**, too!
What has he found for each color?

1 blue whale

**3 yellow
sea horses**

**2 red
starfish**

blue

4 green shells

Take a dive with
Use your
make
sea p

20

Why Can't I Fly?

 shed a little tear

and said, "Why can't I fly?

I want to soar like

Or  through the sky!"

"Every bird is different,"

shouted out.

Find the stickers for the story.

"Some fly, some walk, a  talks,

A  just swims about.

Across the sea flies ,

At night  leaves her nest.

But penguins fly through water,

For that's what they do best!"

23

Toucan's Tasty Trail

1

2

3

Help Toucan follow
the trail of tasty treats.
Use your stickers to put the
fruit in the right circles.

4

5

6

1 2 3 4 5

Birds of a Feather

Add stickers to show:
3 owls
4 hummingbirds
5 seagulls
6 bluebirds

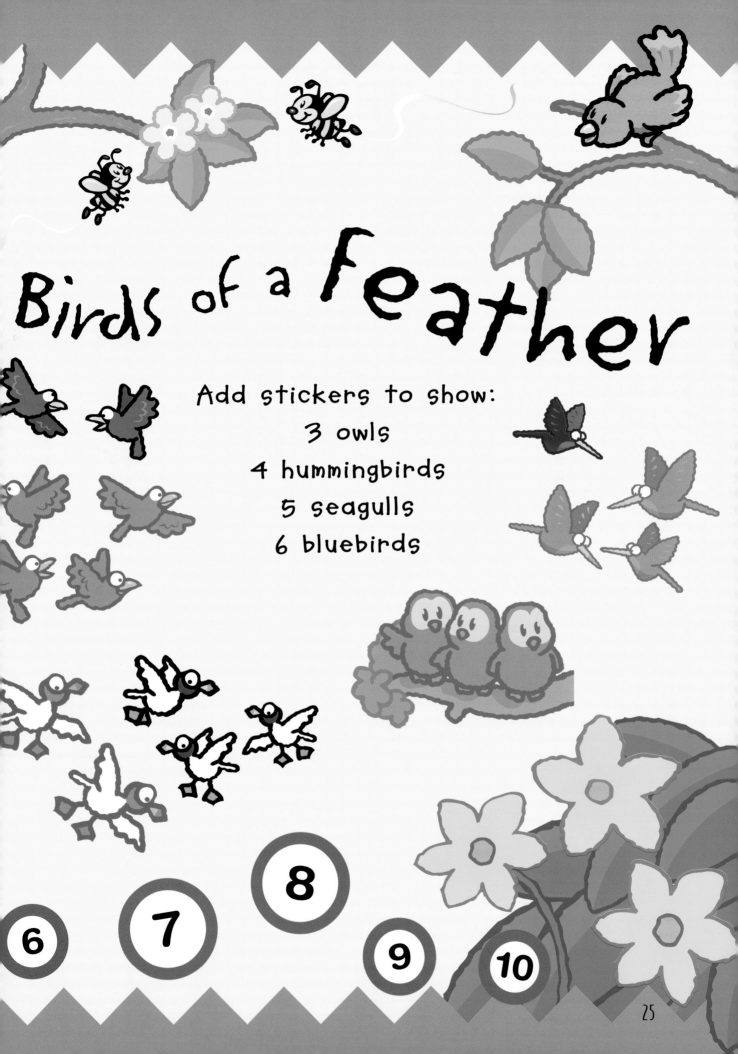

6 7 8 9 10

Find the feathers

All the birds have flown away in a hurry, leaving a flurry of feathers behind!

yellow

black

red

blue

green

white

Find the stickers to match the colors.

Whose feathers are whose? Use your stickers to match the feathers to the right colored birds.

Take to the skies
with Toucan!
Use your stickers
to fill the air with
beautiful birds.

Down on the Farm

It's noisy down on Snappy Farm,

The just loves to MOO.

The big, red, crowing

goes COCK-A-DOODLE-DO!

OINK, OINK, squeals the little

The  just loves to NEIGH.

Find the stickers for the story.

And BAA, BAA, BAA go all the  .

The fat  CLUCKS all day.

But if you hear a  MEOW

Somewhere 'round the house,

You know there is one animal

Being quiet as a...  !

In the
Fields

Pig lives at Snappy Farm, where he has lots of friends. Use your stickers to put the right animals in each field.

sheep

goat

cows

1 **2** **3** **4** **5**

Now count how many animals you can see.

Eggs in the nest

These hens have been busy laying eggs! Give each hen the right number of eggs.

5

8

6

7

6 7 8 9 10

Farmyard Colors

Can you find an animal of each color on Snappy Farm? Who is pink? Who is brown?

white

Find the stickers to match the colors.

brown

pink

red

yellow

black

Join Pig and his friends for
some farmyard fun!
Use your stickers to create
a busy farmyard scene.

Where's my Caterpillar?

I had a ,

but she crawled away.

Perhaps she's asking

or if they can play?

Maybe she's gone with ,

She is so very small.

Find the stickers for the story.

I hope she's not with ,

That wouldn't do at all!

 came zooming past,

A busy  buzzed by,

And then I saw my little friend,

She's now a .

Beetle's Buddies

Add stickers to show
9 ladybugs
10 caterpillars
9 snails
10 grasshoppers

Now count how many bugs you can see.

1 2 3 4 5

Beautiful Butterflies

Beautiful butterflies like to rest on flowers. Are there enough flowers for all of the butterflies? You can use your stickers to find out!

6   7   8   9   10

Snail Race!

The snails are having a race! Who is winning? Who is losing?

Match the snails to the right colored trails.

42

rainbow Colors

Look! There's a rainbow in the sky! Help Bee visit all the flowers in the order hey appear in the rainbow, starting with **red**.

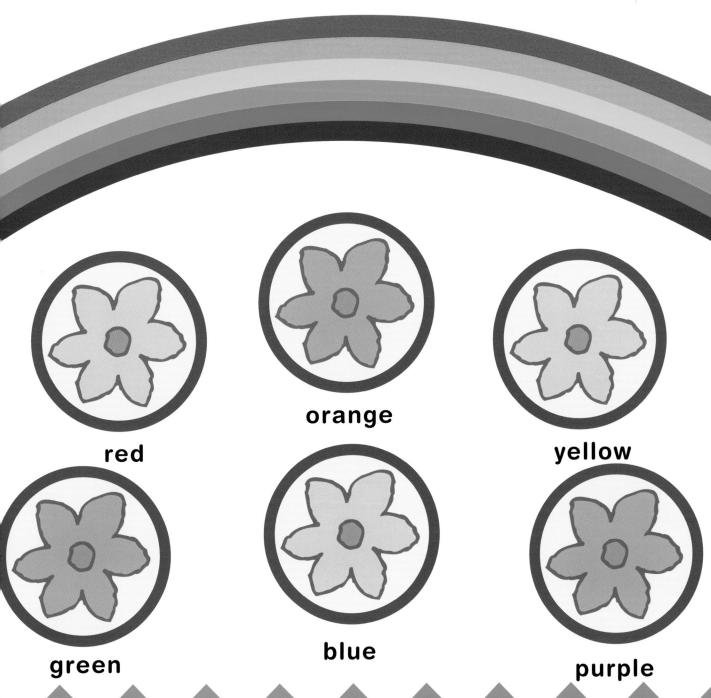

orange

red

yellow

green

blue

purple

Look carefully and you'll find
Beetle and all his friends!
Use your stickers to create
a lively, bug—filled scene!

Now use your stickers to make a pretty beach scene! Can you see Parrot and his friends?

46

How to use your stickers

Look for the page numbers on the sticker sheets to help you find the right stickers for the different activities in this book.

Peel each one carefully from its backing sheet and use it to fill in the shapes or add to the pictures. On some pages, you may need to put your stickers in a particular place to complete an activity. On other pages, you can place your stickers wherever you like!

Don't forget that you can use your stickers again and again, so you can enjoy even more Snappy sticker fun!

stickers for
pages 6 and 7

frog

chameleon

zebra

toucan

monkey

snake

lion

parrot

stickers
for page 8

stickers for
page 9

stickers for
page 10

stickers for page 11

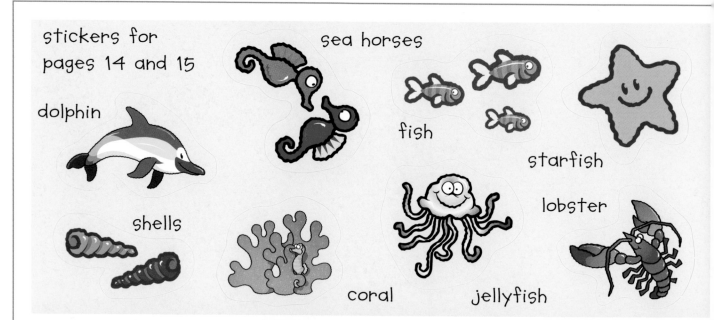

stickers for pages 14 and 15

sea horses

dolphin

fish

starfish

shells

lobster

coral

jellyfish

stickers for page 16

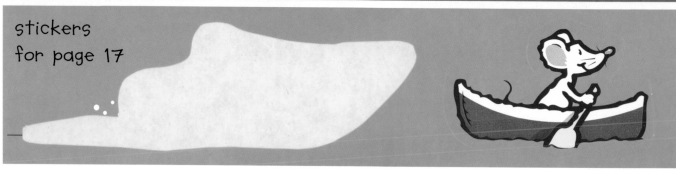

stickers for page 17

more stickers
for page 17

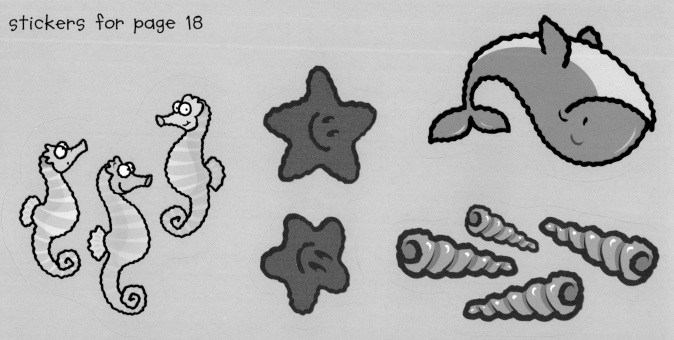

stickers for page 18

stickers for page 19

stickers for pages 22 and 23

owl

penguin

swallow

bluebird

parrot

swan

toucan

seagull

stickers for page 24

stickers for page 25

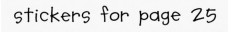

more stickers
for page 25

stickers for
page 26

stickers for
page 27

more stickers for
page 27

stickers for
page 28

stickers for
pages 30 and 31

cow

rooster

horse

pig

hen

sheep

cat

mouse

stickers
for page 32

stickers for
page 33

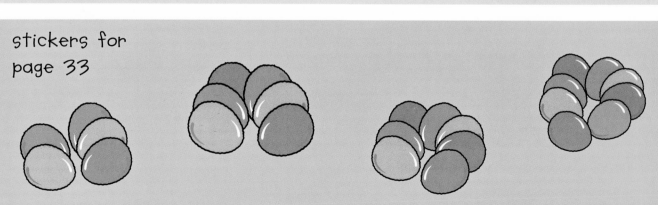

stickers for
pages 36 and 37

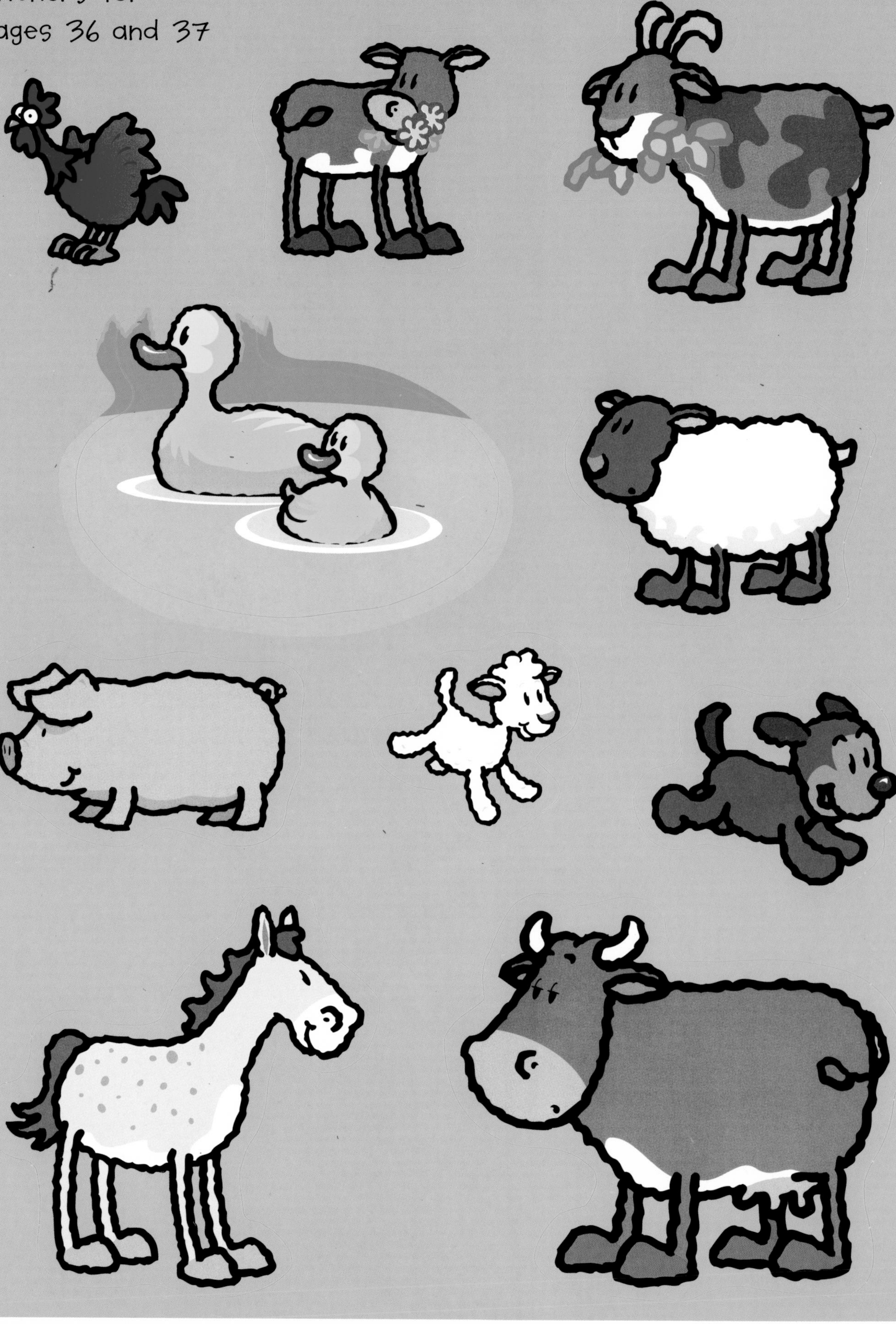

stickers for
pages 38 and 39

caterpillar

ladybug

snail

beetle

spider

dragonfly

bee

butterfly

stickers
for page 40

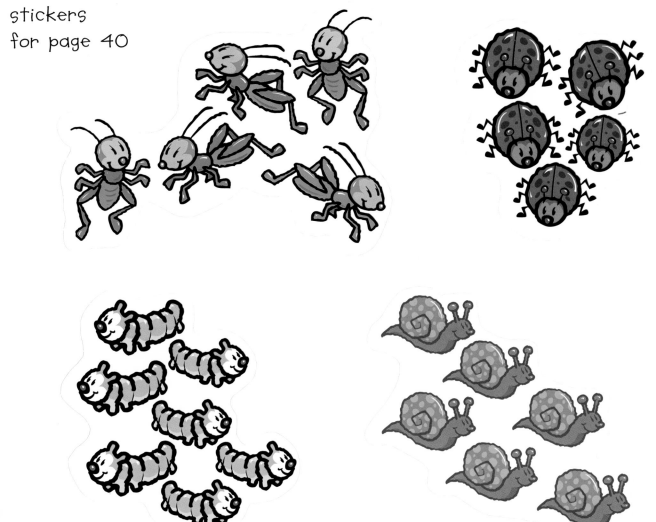

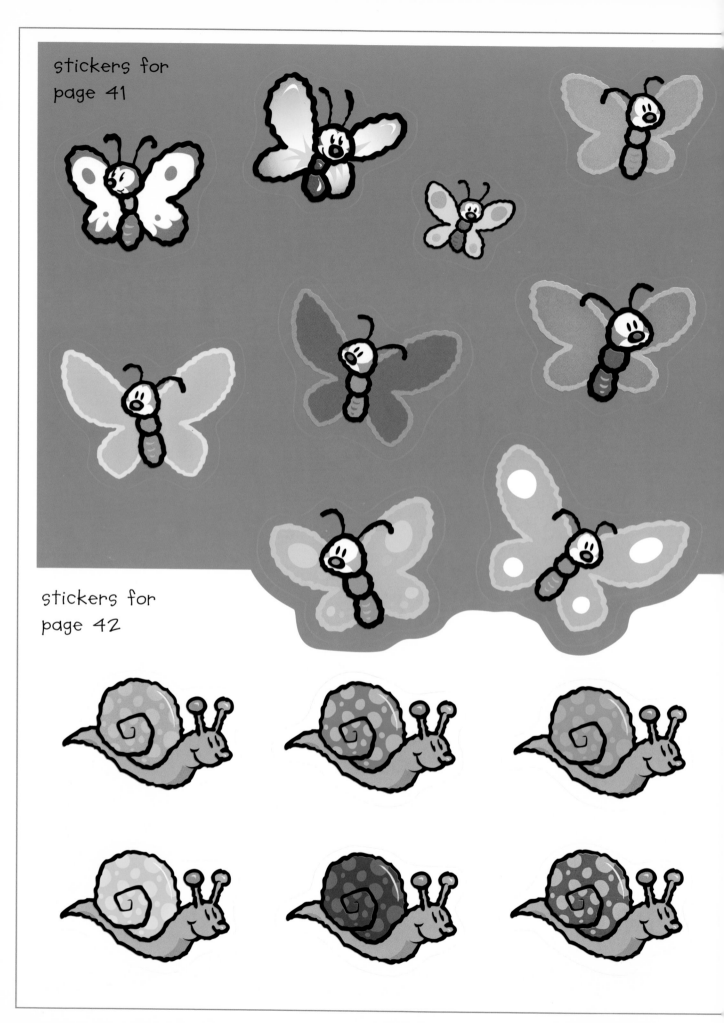

stickers for
page 41

stickers for
page 42

stickers for
page 43

stickers for
pages 44 and 45

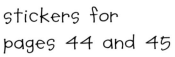